A Guide to
AMERICAN STATES

Kentucky

THE BLUEGRASS STATE

MEDIA ENHANCED BOOKS
AV2 BY WEIGL
ADDED VALUE • AUDIO VISUAL

www.av2books.com

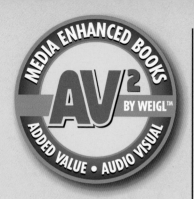

AV² provides enriched content that supplements and complements this book. Weigl's AV² books strive to create inspired learning and engage young minds in a total learning experience.

Your AV² Media Enhanced books come alive with...

Audio
Listen to sections of the book read aloud.

Key Words
Study vocabulary, and complete a matching word activity.

Video
Watch informative video clips.

Quizzes
Test your knowledge.

Go to **www.av2books.com**, and enter this book's unique code.

BOOK CODE

E 7 5 3 9 2 7

Embedded Weblinks
Gain additional information for research.

Slide Show
View images and captions, and prepare a presentation.

AV² by Weigl brings you media enhanced books that support active learning.

Try This!
Complete activities and hands-on experiments.

... and much, much more!

Published by AV² by Weigl
350 5ᵗʰ Avenue, 59ᵗʰ Floor
New York, NY 10118
Website: www.av2books.com   www.weigl.com

Library of Congress Cataloging-in-Publication Data

Evdokimoff, Natasha.
 Kentucky / Natasha Evdokimoff.
    p. cm. -- (A guide to American states)
 Includes index.
 ISBN 978-1-61690-789-1 (hardcover : alk. paper) -- ISBN 978-1-61690-465-4 (online)
 1. Kentucky--Juvenile literature. I. Title.
 F451.3.E933 2011
 976.9--dc22
                          2011018324

Printed in the United States of America in North Mankato, Minnesota

052011
WEP180511

Project Coordinator Jordan McGill
Art Director Terry Paulhus

Photo Credits
Every reasonable effort has been made to trace ownership and to obtain permission to reprint copyright material. The publishers would be pleased to have any errors or omissions brought to their attention so that they may be corrected in subsequent printings.

Weigl acknowledges Getty Images as its primary image supplier for this title.

Contents

Churchill Downs in Louisville is a historic sports venue that hosts the Kentucky Derby and many other horse races.

Introduction

Many people have experienced Kentucky without ever having set foot in the 15th state of the Union. Kentucky has lent its name to numerous renowned events and products, not the least of which is a world-famous **Thoroughbred** horse race. Since 1875 the city of Louisville has hosted the Kentucky Derby, which has been called "the most exciting two minutes in sports."

KFC, a worldwide chain of fast-food restaurants formerly known as Kentucky Fried Chicken, was founded in Corbin. The company is now based in Louisville. Also in Kentucky is the Fort Knox **Bullion** Depository. This heavily guarded building near Louisville holds a large amount of the nation's gold reserves within its vaults.

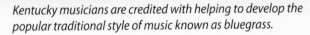
Kentucky musicians are credited with helping to develop the popular traditional style of music known as bluegrass.

The Louisville-based KFC is the most popular chicken restaurant chain in the world.

The fields of the Bluegrass State have been trampled on by many soldiers. The British, American Indians, and American colonists fought for the land during the Revolutionary War in the late 1700s. And because of Kentucky's central location between the North and the South, it was the site of many Civil War battles in the 1860s.

Since the days of the Civil War, Kentucky has fostered a spirit of equality and prosperity. The state has created a vibrant economy, with industries ranging from mining and natural gas production to farming, forestry, and manufacturing. Meanwhile it has maintained the traditions of a style of old-time country music called bluegrass. The state is also known for producing a popular whiskey called bourbon.

With its high-quality products and home-style pleasures, Kentucky has made a name for itself far outside its borders.

Where Is Kentucky?

Kentucky lies in the south-central section of the United States, just east of the Mississippi River. Getting around in Kentucky is quick and easy. The state's extensive road system includes a large network of highways. Railroad transportation in Kentucky began in 1832, and today more than 2,800 miles of railways cross the state. Railroads connect most of Kentucky's major cities and deliver freight to large and small locations. Waterways, such as the Ohio River, play a major role in transporting products in and out of the state.

Louisville is located on the banks of the Ohio River across from Indiana.

Kentucky has a few large cities located around the state. The most populous is Louisville, which is in north-central Kentucky on the Indiana border. The second-largest city, Lexington, is about 75 miles east of Louisville. The state's third-largest city, Owensboro, is in western Kentucky, about 80 miles southwest of Louisville. Bowling Green is in south-central Kentucky, almost 100 miles south of Louisville. Covington is a large suburb of Cincinnati, Ohio, located 95 miles northeast of Louisville.

All of Kentucky's major cities have airports. The Blue Grass Airport in Lexington, the Louisville International Airport, and the Cincinnati/Northern Kentucky International Airport, located near Florence, Kentucky, are the busiest airports in the state.

I DIDN'T KNOW THAT!

Kentucky is nicknamed the Bluegrass State after the bluish-tinted grass that grows throughout its north-central region.

Kentucky's official name is the Commonwealth of Kentucky. The only other **commonwealth** states in the country are Pennsylvania, Virginia, and Massachusetts. Legally, commonwealth states have the same status as other states.

Millions of passengers fly into and out of Cincinnati/Northern Kentucky International Airport each year. The airport is located in Hebron, Kentucky.

Mapping Kentucky

Kentucky is surrounded by no less than seven states. Ohio, Indiana, and Illinois border Kentucky to the north. West Virginia borders Kentucky to the northeast. Missouri is to the west, Virginia to the southeast, and Tennessee to the south. The Ohio River runs the entire length of Kentucky's northern border.

Sites and Symbols

STATE SEAL
Kentucky

STATE BIRD
Cardinal

STATE FLOWER
Goldenrod

STATE FLAG
Kentucky

STATE WILD ANIMAL GAME SPECIES
Gray Squirrel

STATE TREE
Tulip Poplar

Nickname The Bluegrass State

Motto United We Stand, Divided We Fall

Song "My Old Kentucky Home," words and music by Stephen Foster

Entered the Union June 1, 1792, as the 15th state

Capital Frankfort

Population (2010 Census) 4,339,367 Ranked 26th state

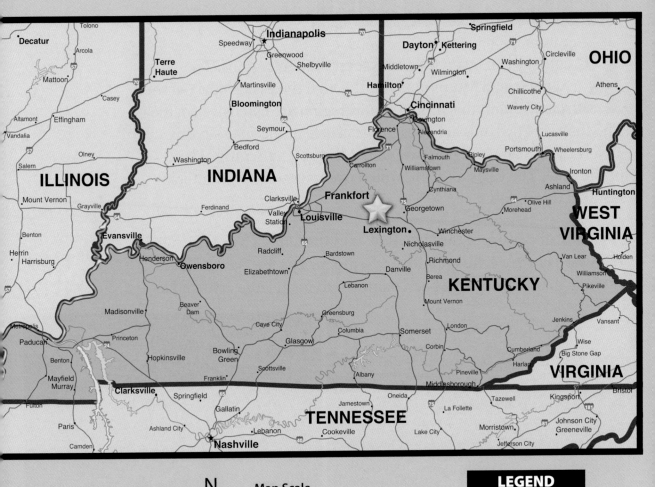

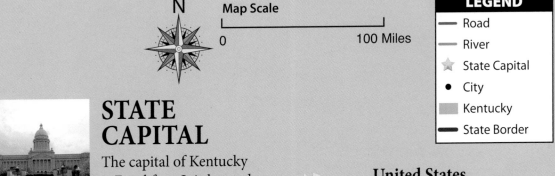

N

Map Scale

0   100 Miles

STATE CAPITAL

The capital of Kentucky is Frankfort. It is located in Franklin County on the Kentucky River, east of Louisville and northwest of Lexington. Frankfort was founded in 1786. It was chosen as the capital by five local commissioners when Kentucky became a state in 1792. The city is the fifth-smallest state capital in the country, with a population of about 27,000.

United States

Hawai'i   Alaska

Kentucky

The Land

Kentucky can be divided into several main regions. The Appalachian Mountains run through the eastern part of the state. Within this mountainous region are extensive coalfields. The Interior Lowlands area lies in the center of the state. In this area is the Bluegrass region, which has the best agricultural land in the state. The Coastal Plain, which occupies western Kentucky, features **floodplains**.

All the major rivers in the state flow into the Ohio River, which is a **tributary** of the Mississippi River. Kentucky has few natural lakes. Instead, many rivers have been dammed to form large artificial lakes.

CUMBERLAND GAP

The Cumberland Gap is the only major pass through the Cumberland Mountains. The natural, narrow pass is 1,650 feet above sea level. An important route for early settlers, it became a national historic park in 1940.

MAMMOTH CAVE NATIONAL PARK

The cave system at Mammoth Cave National Park, located just north of Bowling Green, is the longest in the world. It has more than 360 miles of passageways.

BLUEGRASS REGION

Located in the north-central part of the state, Kentucky's Bluegrass region is a center for Thoroughbred horse breeding. It is named for the bluish-colored grass that covers its miles of rolling hills and pastures.

KENTUCKY LAKE

Kentucky Lake is one of the largest human-made lakes in the world. It has approximately 2,300 miles of shoreline.

The highest point in Kentucky is Big Black Mountain, which stands 4,145 feet above sea level. The peak is located in the Cumberland Mountain range, a section of the Appalachian Mountains that runs along the Kentucky–Virginia border.

Breaks Interstate Park, located in southeastern Kentucky and southwestern Virginia, is sometimes is called the Grand Canyon of the South. In 1767, Daniel Boone became the first person of European heritage to discover the gorge, which he named the Breaks.

The Land Between the Lakes is a national recreational area that is partially in western Kentucky. Located south of Paducah, the massive inland peninsula separates two large human-made bodies of water, Kentucky Lake and Lake Barkley. The 170,000-acre area is teeming with deer and other wildlife.

Trees in Daniel Boone National Forest thrive in the mild climate of eastern Kentucky.

Climate

Kentucky's climate is mild, with warm summers and cool winters. The average annual temperature varies from 52° Fahrenheit in east-central Kentucky to 60° F in the extreme southwest. The average yearly rainfall ranges from about 40 inches in the north to around 55 inches in the south.

The highest temperature ever recorded in Kentucky was 120° F on August 10, 1936, in Ozark. The lowest temperature was –29° F on February 13, 1905, in Brook Farm Pond.

Average Annual Precipitation Across Kentucky

Yearly precipitation can vary greatly in Kentucky depending on location. Why do you think the average precipitation figures are different in Ashland and Bowling Green?

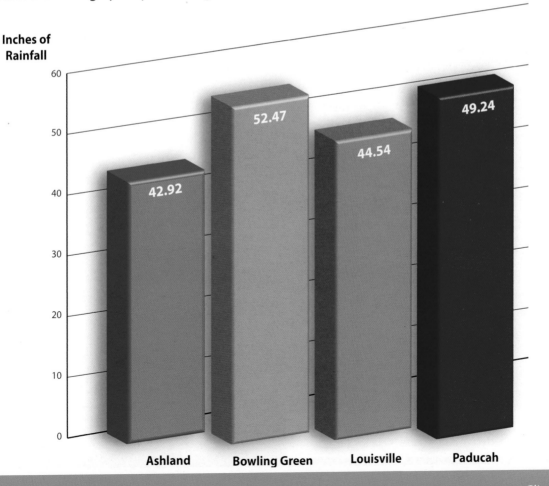

Inches of Rainfall

Ashland	Bowling Green	Louisville	Paducah
42.92	52.47	44.54	49.24

Natural Resources

Kentucky is rich in coal and natural gas deposits. The state is a leading producer of coal in the United States. Each year it typically produces more than 100 million tons of coal, which is mined in both eastern and western Kentucky. Although coal is believed to have been mined in Kentucky since the late 1700s, the state's first commercial coal mine did not open until 1820.

Some Kentucky mine operations remove the tops of hills or mountains to reach coal that is buried near the surface.

Early mining was difficult work. Miners traveled deep into damp, dark tunnels that were covered in coal dust, which is unhealthy to inhale. There was also the risk of mines collapsing. While coal mining continues today, machines now do much of the dangerous work. Coal has been among Kentucky's most important mineral resources for more than a century.

Kentucky has more than 16,000 natural gas wells. Most of them are found in the Big Sandy gas field, in the east. Natural gas is an important energy source used for heating and generating electricity.

Kentucky energy companies use drilling rigs to reach natural gas and petroleum deposits located deep underground.

Coal production has declined a bit in recent years, but Kentucky mines still produce more than 100 million tons of the mineral every year.

Limestone, clay, sand, and gravel are important nonfuel minerals in Kentucky.

Kentucky produces more than 2.6 million barrels of oil each year.

About 12 million acres of forests are found in Kentucky. The state's lumber is used to make furniture and build homes across the country. Commonly harvested Kentucky hardwoods include white oak, tulip poplar, and red oak.

Kentucky has about 1,100 miles of commercially navigable rivers and other waterways. Only Alaska has more.

Plants

Before settlers arrived in the area, Kentucky was almost completely covered by trees. Today nearly half of the state's land is forested. Oak, hickory, ash, walnut, maple, and numerous other hardwood species are commonly found in the state. To help restore the state's forest cover, millions of trees are planted each year in Kentucky.

Small plants also thrive in the state. Flowering shrubs, such as the azalea and the mountain laurel, are common. Many beautiful wildflowers, including the violet, bluebell, and lady's slipper, also bloom across the state. Patches of the state flower, the goldenrod, provide a colorful display every fall.

KENTUCKY LADY'S SLIPPERS

Kentucky lady's slippers are orchids that can be found in the eastern part of the state. The flowers grow in hardwood forests in damp, low-lying areas, and they bloom from April through June.

TULIP POPLAR TREES

The tulip poplar is the official state tree. Also known as the yellow poplar or the tulip tree, it can grow to nearly 200 feet tall.

GOLDENRODS

The goldenrod was adopted as the state flower of Kentucky in 1926. It grows wild across the state.

KENTUCKY COFFEE TREES

The Kentucky coffee tree was Kentucky's state tree from 1976 to 1994. This rare tree was given its name because early settlers used its seeds to make a coffee substitute.

Sugar maples are slow-growing hardwood trees that can reach a height of 130 feet or more. They can be found everywhere in Kentucky except for the extreme southwest.

Blackberries are Kentucky's official state fruit. Blackberry plants grow throughout the state, as well as in the rest of the temperate areas of the Northern Hemisphere.

Animals

Kentucky's forests are filled with many kinds of wild animals. Deer are frequently seen roaming the land. Smaller Kentucky creatures include the beaver, fox, mink, muskrat, raccoon, and woodchuck. The state's numerous caves have a thriving bat population.

Kentucky's trees are home to a variety of birds. Cardinals, sparrows, and orioles fill the air with their songs. **Migratory** birds flock to the state to visit the floodplains in the state's northwest corner. This part of Kentucky lies along one of the world's great migratory bird routes. Snipes, mourning doves, and warblers are among the many birds that pass through the state. In the marshes of southwestern Kentucky are found the American egret, great blue heron, and double-crested cormorant.

GRAY FOX

The gray fox is normally found in mixed hardwood forests. It is adept at climbing trees and often uses this skill to escape when being hunted.

CARDINAL

The cardinal is the official state bird of Kentucky. Cardinals are a type of finch found in gardens, woodlands, and thickets throughout the eastern and southern United States.

VICEROY BUTTERFLY

The viceroy butterfly is Kentucky's state butterfly. It lives in meadows, marshes, swamps, and other wet regions.

GREAT BLUE HERON

This large wading bird can grow to be more than four feet tall from head to tail and can have a wingspan of more than six feet.

Through restoration efforts, Kentucky's wild turkey population has grown from fewer than 1,000 in the mid-1950s to more than 200,000 today.

Common carp are found in reservoirs and lakes throughout Kentucky. Many other fish also frequent the state's waters, including bluegill, largemouth bass, channel catfish, and longnose gar.

Tourism

One of Kentucky's most visited attractions is a small log cabin near Hodgenville that marks the birthplace of Abraham Lincoln. Although the original cabin no longer exists, a similar one built in the early 1900s serves as its substitute. At age 7, Lincoln moved with his family to Indiana. He later lived in Illinois before becoming the 16th president of the United States.

Churchill Downs in Louisville is a first-class horse-racing facility that attracts many visitors. The most famous race at the track is the annual Kentucky Derby. More than 150,000 people travel to Churchill Downs on Derby day, which takes place on the first Saturday in May.

Kentucky also is home to more than 50 state parks. From recreational lakes and mountain areas to sites that celebrate Kentucky's history, tourists have plenty of interesting things to do in the state.

ABRAHAM LINCOLN BIRTHPLACE

This National Historic Park, located near Hodgenville, features a memorial that houses a replica of the cabin in which Lincoln was born. It also includes a small log house at a separate site nearby, Knob Creek, where Lincoln lived from age 2 to 7.

CHURCHILL DOWNS

World-class Thoroughbred racing is this famous Louisville attraction's main draw, but Churchill Downs also offers tours of its stables and a museum celebrating the history of the Kentucky Derby.

CUMBERLAND FALLS STATE RESORT PARK

This park, in southeastern Kentucky, features a 68-foot waterfall that sometimes is called the Niagara of the South. People who visit Cumberland Falls when the moon is full can witness a moonbow, which is a rainbow created when moonlight hits water vapor from the falls.

KENTUCKY HORSE PARK

This Lexington attraction is both an educational theme park and a working farm. Horse competitions also are held at the facility, which spreads out over more than 1,200 acres in Kentucky's Bluegrass region. Visitors can observe about 50 breeds of horse on the park's grounds.

I DIDN'T KNOW THAT!

Each year tourists spend more than $10 billion in Kentucky.

Big South Fork National River and Recreation Area offers plenty of scenic views and outdoor activities. The popular tourist destination is situated on 125,000 acres along the Kentucky-Tennessee border.

The National Corvette Museum in Bowling Green features a variety of exhibits dedicated to the popular sports car.

Louisville gears up for the Kentucky Derby with the annual Kentucky Derby Festival. During the two weeks leading up to the race, about 1.5 million people attend the festival, which features more than 70 events.

Industry

Kentucky's economy is made up of a number of different industries. Agriculture is an important source of income for the state. Although most farms in the state are small in size by national standards, Kentucky farms produce more than $2 billion for the state every year. Tobacco is one of the leading crops. In fact, only North Carolina produces more tobacco. Burley is the most common type of tobacco grown in Kentucky, accounting for more than 70 percent of the state's tobacco harvest.

Industries in Kentucky
Value of Goods and Services in Millions of Dollars

Government is one of the most important sectors of the Kentucky economy. Can you name some jobs that government workers do?

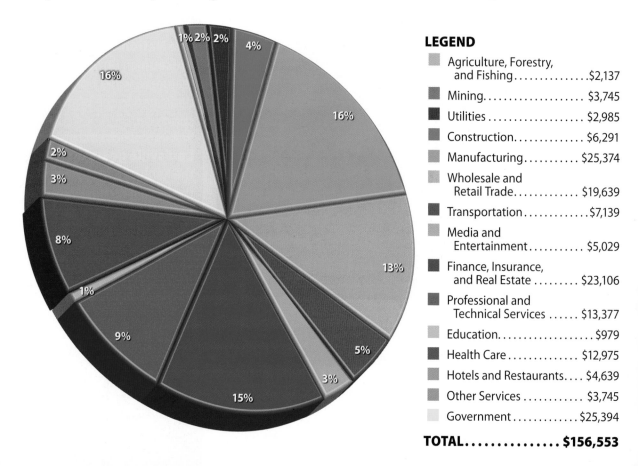

LEGEND

Agriculture, Forestry, and Fishing	$2,137
Mining	$3,745
Utilities	$2,985
Construction	$6,291
Manufacturing	$25,374
Wholesale and Retail Trade	$19,639
Transportation	$7,139
Media and Entertainment	$5,029
Finance, Insurance, and Real Estate	$23,106
Professional and Technical Services	$13,377
Education	$979
Health Care	$12,975
Hotels and Restaurants	$4,639
Other Services	$3,745
Government	$25,394
TOTAL	**$156,553**

Kentucky produces about 200 million pounds of tobacco each year.

There are about 85,000 farms in Kentucky. The average size of a Kentucky farm is 164 acres.

The famed Louisville Slugger baseball bat was first made in 1884. Although most of the bats are now manufactured elsewhere, a museum honoring the Louisville Slugger is located in Louisville.

Annual shipments of transportation equipment manufactured in Kentucky are valued at nearly $30 million.

Soybeans, which are grown in western Kentucky, are another valuable crop. Corn, wheat, hay, vegetables, and fruit are also important.

Kentucky is a manufacturing center for transportation equipment. Sports cars, trucks, and automotive parts are made in the state. Industrial machinery and electronic equipment are also manufactured in Kentucky. The production of chemicals has grown in significance.

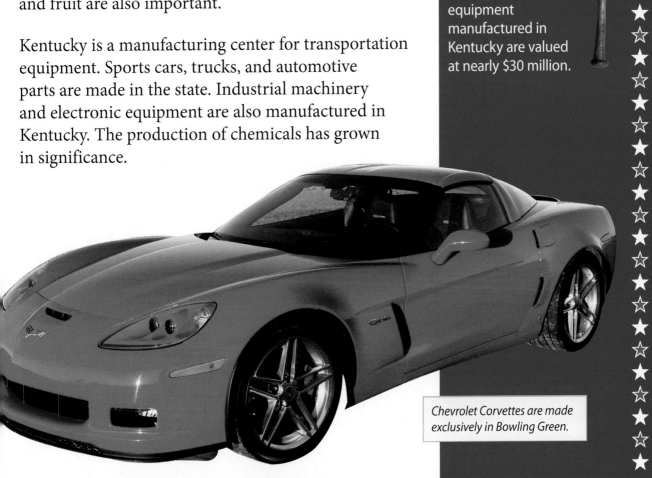

Chevrolet Corvettes are made exclusively in Bowling Green.

Goods and Services

Using its abundant natural resources, Kentucky produces a large amount of electricity. Coal-fired power stations provide more than 90 percent of the state's electricity. Water is also used to make electricity in the state. Large **hydroelectric** plants are found on the Ohio, Cumberland, and Tennessee rivers. In addition, Kentucky's river systems are important gateways to trade, providing transportation to markets outside the state.

Kentucky is the nation's leading producer of Thoroughbreds. Horse breeding began in the state before 1800. Once Churchill Downs opened in 1875, the breeding of Thoroughbreds became an important part of the state's economy. Many colts are raised to become contenders in the Kentucky Derby or to participate in show events. Others are sold to horse lovers around the world. The state's several Thoroughbred racetracks also contribute to the economy.

Barges use the Ohio River to transport a wide variety of goods to and from Kentucky.

Kentucky has more Thoroughbred horse farms than anywhere else in the world.

A majority of the workers in Kentucky are employed in service industries, such as retail trade, transportation, finance and insurance, and food service. Many people in the state work for the government or the military or work in health care or education.

Those who want a college education have many schools to choose from in Kentucky. Approximately 270,000 students attend colleges and universities in the state. Founded in 1789, Transylvania University in Lexington is the oldest university west of the Allegheny Mountains. Also in Lexington is the University of Kentucky, the state's largest university. The University of Louisville, which was founded in 1798, is the state's oldest public university.

Kentucky has a strong military presence at Fort Knox, near Louisville. Many U.S. troops trained for combat on these grounds in preparation for World War II. On the base, a museum showcases equipment, vehicles, and artifacts that highlight the history of U.S. armor units and **cavalry**. The museum also features items that once belonged to World War II hero General George Patton.

I DIDN'T KNOW THAT!

Thoroughbred horses are the fastest horses in the world. They can achieve speeds of up to 45 miles per hour.

Tourism is an important industry in the state, employing more than 160,000 Kentuckians.

About $6 billion in gold is stored in the vaults at the Fort Knox Bullion Depository. Within the building is a vault door that weighs more than 20 tons.

Bourbon, a type of whiskey, was developed in Kentucky in the late 1700s. Today the state produces nearly all the bourbon made in the world.

Kentucky is home to the nation's oldest printing house for the blind.

American Indians

Archaeologists have found evidence showing that American Indians have been living in what is now Kentucky for as long as 12,000 years. Ancient artifacts reveal that several different American Indian groups thrived in the area.

Shawnee Indians typically lived in small round dwellings called wigwams.

A wooden monument in Paducah honors the Chickasaw Indians that used to live in the area.

In the 1670s the Shawnee were driven out of Kentucky, possibly by the Iroquois, but they later returned.

Some American Indians left after the arrival of Europeans, but many stayed in the region, determined to keep their land. They engaged in so many battles with early settlers that Kentucky became known as the "dark and bloody ground."

The Cherokee Trail of Tears park in Hopkinsville commemorates the forced journey Cherokee Indians made in 1838 and 1839 from the southeastern U.S. to Indian Territory west of the Mississippi River.

More than 11,000 American Indians make their home in Kentucky.

Shawnee chief Kishkalwa visited Washington, D.C., in 1825 with a delegation of other Indian leaders. When he was young, he was said to have led many skillful attacks against enemy tribesmen in Kentucky.

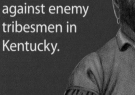

The prehistoric Indians were hunters who lived in small groups, traveling in search of game, such as bison. Later, American Indians began to make woven baskets, stone tools, and clay pottery. Evidence of an American Indian group known as the Mound Builders can still be seen along the Ohio River. These people created large mounds of earth that were often used for burials. Agriculture began to gain importance to the Indians, who started cultivating crops such as corn and beans. Other groups eventually entered the area, including the Shawnee, Chickasaw, Iroquois, and Cherokee. Fighting often broke out between the tribes, and by the mid-1700s the largest tribe left in the area was the Shawnee.

Daniel Boone helped build the road known as the Wilderness Trail and led settlers through the Cumberland Gap into the Kentucky area, which he called a "second paradise."

Explorers

In 1674 a British explorer named Gabriel Arthur became the first known European to enter the Kentucky region. In 1682 René-Robert Cavelier, sieur de La Salle, claimed the entire Mississippi Valley, which included Kentucky, for France. For most of the next 100 years, France and Great Britain fought for control of eastern North America, until France was forced to give up almost all of the land it had claimed east of the Mississippi River.

Extensive exploration of the Kentucky area was slowed by the Appalachian Mountains, which made it difficult to enter the region from the east. Attempts to investigate Kentucky intensified, however, after British officials began offering land grants in the region. Scouts were sent to search for possible settlement locations.

In 1750 Dr. Thomas Walker of the Loyal Land Company led a group of Virginians into Kentucky through a pass in the Cumberland Mountains. He named it the Cumberland Gap, and its discovery sparked a rush of hunters and settlers. Many of these early adventurers stayed in Kentucky so long that they were called long hunters. Daniel Boone was one of the early long hunters.

Timeline of Settlement

Early Exploration

1750 Dr. Thomas Walker takes the first surveying party into Kentucky, through the Cumberland Gap.

1751 Christopher Gist explores the Ohio River.

1754–1763 After the French and Indian War, France surrenders land, including what is now Kentucky, to Britain.

1769 Daniel Boone visits Kentucky in 1767. He returns in 1769 with a group of hunters for a two-year exploration.

First Settlements

1774 The first permanent settlement in Kentucky is constructed at Fort Harrod.

1775 Daniel Boone establishes Fort Boonesborough, and many other settlements are created soon after.

Revolutionary War and Statehood

1776 Kentucky is made a separate county of the state of Virginia after the American colonies declare their independence.

1792 On June 1 Kentucky becomes the 15th state to join the Union. Isaac Shelby is elected as Kentucky's first governor.

1818 The far west region of Kentucky now called the Jackson Purchase, is added to the state after it is bought from the Chickasaw Indians.

Civil War

1861–1865 Kentucky is torn by conflicting loyalties when the Civil War erupts. The state officially declares itself neutral, although several southern Kentucky counties join the Confederacy. Forty-thousand Kentucky citizens fight for the South and 100,000 for the North. The war ends with a Union victory.

Early Settlers

Although he was born in Pennsylvania, Daniel Boone is known as a Kentucky pioneer. Boone came to Kentucky through the Cumberland Gap with a group of explorers in 1775. They blazed a trail through the wilderness and established a fort that became known as Boonesborough.

Map of Settlements and Resources in Early Kentucky

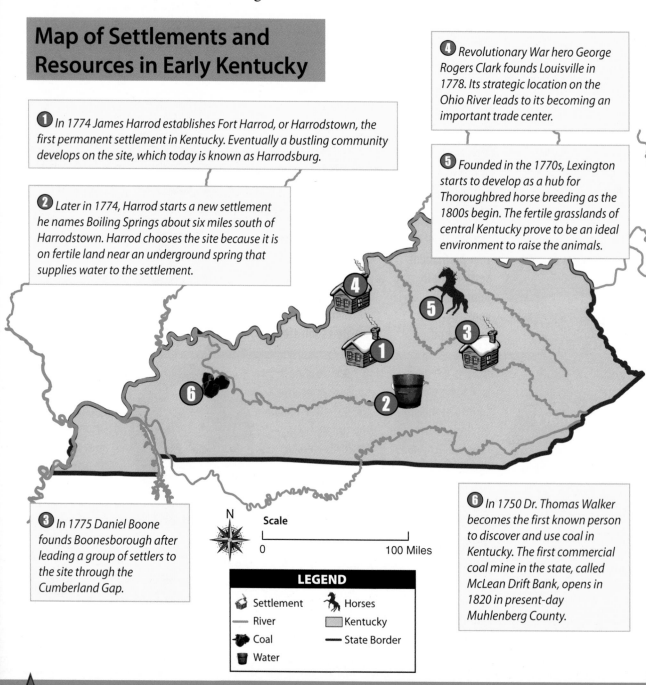

1 In 1774 James Harrod establishes Fort Harrod, or Harrodstown, the first permanent settlement in Kentucky. Eventually a bustling community develops on the site, which today is known as Harrodsburg.

2 Later in 1774, Harrod starts a new settlement he names Boiling Springs about six miles south of Harrodstown. Harrod chooses the site because it is on fertile land near an underground spring that supplies water to the settlement.

4 Revolutionary War hero George Rogers Clark founds Louisville in 1778. Its strategic location on the Ohio River leads to its becoming an important trade center.

5 Founded in the 1770s, Lexington starts to develop as a hub for Thoroughbred horse breeding as the 1800s begin. The fertile grasslands of central Kentucky prove to be an ideal environment to raise the animals.

3 In 1775 Daniel Boone founds Boonesborough after leading a group of settlers to the site through the Cumberland Gap.

6 In 1750 Dr. Thomas Walker becomes the first known person to discover and use coal in Kentucky. The first commercial coal mine in the state, called McLean Drift Bank, opens in 1820 in present-day Muhlenberg County.

N

Scale

0   100 Miles

LEGEND

Settlement		Horses	
River		Kentucky	
Coal		State Border	
Water			

After attempts to establish Kentucky as a separate colony failed, the region was made a county of Virginia in 1776. During the American Revolution, the Shawnee, who were allies of the British, led many attacks on Kentucky settlements. One of the largest attacks was on Boonesborough in 1778. Daniel Boone organized the defense of Boonesborough, and the town withstood a 10-day siege.

After the Revolution, Kentucky County experienced a massive migration of settlers from the eastern regions of the country. With this growth came demands for independence from Virginia. Finally, on June 1, 1792, Kentucky became the 15th state of the Union.

During the early 1800s, as settlers continued to move to Kentucky, more and more wilderness was transformed into farmland. Tobacco became an important crop for Kentucky farmers. Horse breeders also began moving to the state when it was discovered that the fertile pastures of central Kentucky were ideal for raising horses.

When tensions developed within the United States over the issue of slavery, Kentucky tried to remain neutral. When the Civil War erupted, however, neither the Union nor the Confederacy respected Kentucky's neutrality. Many battles were fought on the state's soil.

Tobacco farming became important to Kentucky before the Civil War and remains a valuable industry for the state today.

I DIDN'T KNOW THAT!

Dr. Thomas Walker was unimpressed with the region, and the Loyal Land Company never settled any lands in Kentucky.

Land speculator Richard Henderson became one of the state's original founders when the Virginia legislature granted him 200,000 acres of Kentucky land in the 1770s. He also organized the Transylvania Company, which hired Daniel Boone to **blaze** the historic trail through the Cumberland Gap.

In 1778 Daniel Boone was captured by American Indians and was adopted as a son by the Shawnee chief Blackfish. Boone was able to escape after five months.

The last battle of the American Revolution was fought at Blue Licks (near Mount Olivet) in 1782.

Between 1775 and 1810, an estimated 200,000 to 300,000 people traveled through the Cumberland Gap into Kentucky.

By 1860 Kentucky's population was more than 1 million. Nearly one quarter of the people living in the state were slaves.

Notable People

Many people who were born and lived in Kentucky have contributed to the rich history of the state and the country. From explorers to politicians to business people, Kentuckians, through their deeds and accomplishments, have left their mark on history.

DANIEL BOONE
(1734–1820)

The Pennsylvania-born Boone's trail-blazing trips into the Kentucky wilderness paved the way for settlement of the region by people from east of the Appalachians. Boone's explorations of Kentucky began in 1767, and in 1775 he helped clear a trail through the Cumberland Gap that became the major route into the area. That same year he established the early Kentucky settlement of Boonesborough. Following the American Revolution, he held several government posts. He moved away from Kentucky in 1788 but returned in 1795. From 1799 on, he mainly lived in what is now Missouri.

HENRY CLAY
(1777–1852)

Clay, who settled in Kentucky around 1797, was a leading American political figure during the first half of the 19th century. He served in the U.S. Congress for more than 30 years. He also was secretary of state from 1825 to 1829 under President John Quincy Adams. Clay became known as the Great Compromiser for his attempts to resolve growing tensions between the North and South.

ZACHARY TAYLOR (1784–1850)

Raised in Louisville, Taylor went on to have a 40-year career in the U.S. Army. He became a national hero when he led his forces to two major victories during the Mexican-American War. In 1848 Taylor was elected the 12th U.S. president, but his time in office was short. He died in 1850, shortly after becoming ill at a July 4th celebration.

LOUIS BRANDEIS (1856–1941)

This Louisville native became the first Jewish person to serve on the U.S. Supreme Court. He was appointed to the Court in 1916 and spent 23 years as a justice. Brandeis was known as a supporter of social and economic reforms and as a defender of individual liberties. Brandeis University in Massachusetts was named for him.

JUANITA KREPS (1921–2010)

Kreps, who was born in Lynch, was the first woman to serve as U.S. secretary of commerce. She held the post from 1977 to 1979. During that time, Kreps helped negotiate a historic trade agreement with China. She also was known for supporting programs to protect the environment and to aid women, the unemployed, and minority-owned businesses.

I DIDN'T KNOW THAT!

Carrie Nation (1846–1911), who was from Garrard County, gained notoriety later in life for her anti-alcohol protests in Kansas and Missouri. The devout Christian was known for entering saloons and smashing up liquor bottles with a hatchet.

Harland Sanders (1890–1980) opened a café in 1929 in the back of his service station in Corbin. He perfected a fried chicken recipe there that he used to start Kentucky Fried Chicken. Colonel Sanders, as he was called, became famous as the spokesman of the fast-food chain, which is now known as KFC.

Population

Kentucky had a population of more than 4.3 million people at the time of the 2010 U.S. Census. From 2000 to 2010 the state's population grew by more than 7 percent. During the 1800s and early 1900s, most Kentuckians lived in **rural** areas, many working as farmers. After 1960 more of the population began to move into **urban** centers in search of better jobs. Today more than half of Kentucky's residents are city dwellers.

Kentucky Population 1950–2010

Since 1950, Kentucky's population has increased during each 10-year period. In some decades growth has been slow. In other decades the population increase has been much greater. What are some reasons why the rate of population increase might change from one decade to another?

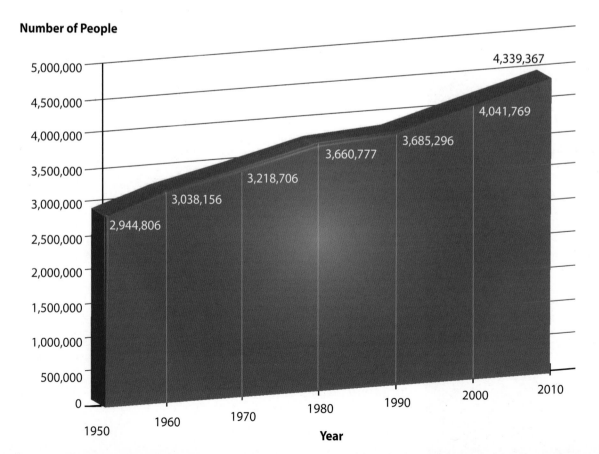

Number of People

- 2,944,806 (1950)
- 3,038,156 (1960)
- 3,218,706 (1970)
- 3,660,777 (1980)
- 3,685,296 (1990)
- 4,041,769 (2000)
- 4,339,367 (2010)

Year

About 42 percent of Kentucky's population lives in rural areas.

I DIDN'T KNOW THAT!

There are 120 counties in Kentucky.

Louisville was named in honor of King Louis XVI of France.

Louisville and Lexington, Kentucky's two most populous cities, have estimated populations of about 567,000 and 297,000, respectively.

Even though the state has several large cities, Kentucky has retained its small-town charm. Quiet tourist communities and smaller college towns are found throughout the state, providing Kentucky with a pleasant and low-key atmosphere. Louisville and Lexington are the state's most populous cities. Other notable cities include Owensboro, Bowling Green, and Covington.

Residents and tourists alike are drawn by the thousands to Churchill Downs in Louisville, Kentucky's largest city, to watch the Kentucky Derby.

Kentucky's State Capitol combines Greek and French architectural styles. It is the fourth building since 1792 to be used as the Capitol.

Politics and Government

There are three branches of the Kentucky state government. They are the executive branch, the legislative branch, and the judicial branch. The executive branch is led by the governor. It ensures that state laws and state business are carried out correctly. The legislative branch passes new laws and has the power to change old ones. The judicial branch is made up of the court system, in which legal cases are tried. The state's highest court is the Kentucky Supreme Court. It has seven justices, or judges, who are elected to eight-year terms.

Frankfort is Kentucky's state capital. The city, which was founded in 1786, is where the state legislature meets. The legislature has two chambers, or parts. The Senate is made up of 38 senators, and the House of Representatives has 100 members.

Albert Benjamin "Happy" Chandler was Kentucky's governor during the 1930s and the 1950s. He also was a U.S. senator from 1939 to 1945, as well as the Commissioner of Baseball from 1945 to 1951.

Cultural Groups

Kentucky has a rich folk tradition. The state was first settled by people of English, Scottish, and Irish heritage. Descendants of these early settlers live in the state today, and some of them work hard to preserve their European heritage. Cultural festivals, such as the Highland Games in Glasgow, keep Scottish traditions alive. For four days every spring descendants of Kentucky's early Scottish settlers compete in traditional music and sporting events. The harp events and highland dancing competitions are popular attractions. Many of the competitors wear traditional Scottish kilts, which display their family plaid.

Bluegrass music is a unique feature of Kentucky's folk culture. A type of country music, it originated in the Bluegrass and Appalachian regions. Bluegrass music is strongly influenced by jazz and the blues. Many of its songs tell sad tales of lost love and loneliness. Traditional bluegrass instruments include the banjo, guitar, **mandolin**, and fiddle. Bluegrass festivals are held throughout the year in Kentucky. Some festivals feature several days of music.

The Glasgow Highland Games are one of three annual events celebrating Scottish heritage in Kentucky. The others are the Kentucky Scottish Weekend in Carrollton and the Western Kentucky Highland Festival in Murray.

Bluegrass pioneer Bill Monroe (1911-1996) sold more than 50 million records during a career that spanned some six decades.

Bill Monroe, who was born in Rosine in 1911, has been called the Father of Bluegrass Music. He played the mandolin in his band, the Blue Grass Boys, which helped introduce Kentucky's brand of bluegrass music to the world. The band's most famous song was "Blue Moon of Kentucky."

The Shakers were once a distinct **communal** society in Kentucky. This religious group settled in the state during the late 1700s. The Shakers believed that they could become closer to God through intense prayer. They held lengthy meetings and often became so involved in their prayers that they shook, which is how their name originated. The Shakers were well known for their labor-saving inventions and high-quality furniture. In the late 1800s the group slowly began to disappear. Today tourists can visit the Shaker Village of Pleasant Hill, where actors in costume demonstrate how Shakers lived. This village is located on 2,800 acres and features more than 30 buildings from the 1800s.

I DIDN'T KNOW THAT!

The Folklife Festival is held annually in Frankfort and celebrates the diverse ethnic backgrounds of the state's people.

Bowling Green hosts the annual International Festival, which highlights cultures from around the world.

The mid-1800s brought a wave of German immigrants to the state. German culture is still celebrated in Kentucky, especially in the north. Annual cultural events include Oktoberfest.

Kentucky's mountain communities are home to many talented furniture makers and craftspeople. The town of Berea has more than 40 craft shops full of handmade items. In fact, Berea is known as the Folk Arts and Crafts Capital of Kentucky.

The National Quilt Museum is located in Paducah.

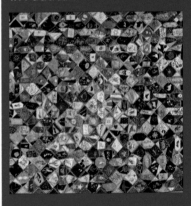

Arts and Entertainment

Many popular entertainers were born in Kentucky. One of the best known is the country and western singer Loretta Lynn. Born in Butcher Hollow in 1935, Lynn was the second of eight children from a poor coal-mining family. She became known for her songs that dealt with problems facing women in rural America. Lynn was the first female country singer to have a certified gold album.

The mother-daughter duo of Naomi and Wynonna Judd is another popular country music act from the state. The Judds, who both were born in Ashland, have had more than a dozen number-one country hits.

Other Kentuckians who made their mark in country music include Crystal Gayle, Dwight Yoakam, and the duo Montgomery Gentry. In addition, the state is the birthplace of jazz icon Lionel Hampton, who was born in Louisville in 1908. A musician and bandleader, he was best known for his work on the **vibraphone**.

The Judds have released six albums that have sold more than 1 million copies in the United States.

The Everly Brothers were a popular Kentucky music duo in the 1950s and early 1960s. Don Everly was born in Brownie in 1937, and his brother Phil was born in the same town in 1939. Among their most famous rock-and-roll songs are "Bye Bye Love" and "Wake Up Little Susie."

Kentucky has also produced a number of notable writers, including Robert Penn Warren. In 1986 he became the country's first poet laureate. William Wells Brown, who was born in Lexington in about 1814, is believed to have been the first African American to publish a novel. His popular autobiography, *Narrative of William W. Brown, a Fugitive Slave*, was released in 1847.

Classical music lovers attend performances by the Kentucky Symphony Orchestra and the Louisville Orchestra. Kentucky also has a well-respected ballet company based in Lexington.

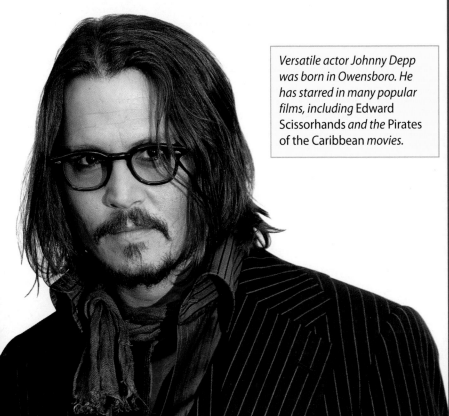

Versatile actor Johnny Depp was born in Owensboro. He has starred in many popular films, including Edward Scissorhands *and the* Pirates of the Caribbean *movies.*

Singer Loretta Lynn's autobiography, *Coal Miner's Daughter*, was made into an acclaimed movie in 1980.

The Everly Brothers' early style of rock and roll influenced countless bands, including the Beatles.

The Country Music Highway in eastern Kentucky was named after the many country musicians who were born in the state.

Oscar-winning movie star George Clooney was born in Lexington and grew up in Augusta.

The Pioneer Playhouse was founded in Danville in 1950. It is the oldest outdoor theater in Kentucky.

Sports

One of the greatest sports legends of all time is from Kentucky. Muhammad Ali, who was born Cassius Clay in Louisville in 1942, became the world's most renowned boxer. At the age of 22, he changed his name after converting to Islam. Known for his strength and agility, he was the first boxer to win the heavyweight title three times. Ali, whose motto was "I am the greatest," dominated the sport of boxing for nearly two decades.

Equestrian sports are extremely popular in Kentucky. In addition to Thoroughbred racing, horseback-riding competitions called eventing attract large audiences. Eventing competitions test horses and riders in three areas. They are **dressage**, cross-country riding, and show jumping. The Rolex Kentucky Three-Day Event, held at the Kentucky Horse Park in Lexington, is one of the top eventing competitions in the world.

Kentucky is the perfect place for those who love the outdoors. Spots for camping, hiking, horseback riding, and biking are plentiful in the state. Water sports are enjoyed at many of Kentucky's lakes. The state's dense forests are ideal for hunting, while fishing enthusiasts take advantage of the well-stocked rivers and streams. Kentucky is also known for its deep caves. Cave explorers, or spelunkers, probe into the damp darkness in search of interesting rock formations. Many of Kentucky's caves are thousands of years old.

Prior to his successful professional boxing career, Muhammad Ali won a gold medal at the 1960 Olympics. Since retiring, he has focused on supporting various charities and promoting peace.

The University of Kentucky Wildcats men's basketball team has won seven national championships, second to only UCLA's 11 titles.

Adolph Rupp was the head coach of the Kentucky Wildcats men's basketball team from 1930 to 1972. One of the most successful college basketball coaches, he led the team to 879 victories and also to four national championships.

Brothers Darrell and Michael Waltrip are successful NASCAR race car drivers who were born in Owensboro. Both have won the prestigious Daytona 500 race, Darrell in 1989 and Michael in 2001 and 2003.

Muhammad Ali claimed that his boxing style was to "float like a butterfly, sting like a bee."

Louisville-born Rajon Rondo is a pro basketball player who helped the Boston Celtics win the NBA Championship in 2008.

Eventing competitions grew out of training tests for military horses.

Many Kentuckians are fans of college sports. Basketball is one of the most popular college sports in the state. The Universities of Louisville and Kentucky are especially known for their legions of faithful fans. Kentucky's strong fan base attracts some of the best players and coaches to the state's university and college teams. As a result, Kentucky's basketball teams have enjoyed season after season of success. By 2010 the University of Kentucky Wildcats men's basketball team had won seven national championships.

National Averages Comparison

T he United States is a federal republic, consisting of fifty states and the District of Columbia. Alaska and Hawai'i are the only non-contiguous, or non-touching, states in the nation. Today, the United States of America is the third-largest country in the world in population. The United States Census Bureau takes a census, or count of all the people, every ten years. It also regularly collects other kinds of data about the population and the economy. How does Kentucky compare to the national average?

Comparison Chart

United States 2010 Census Data *	USA	Kentucky
Admission to Union	NA	June 15, 1836
Land Area (in square miles)	3,537,438.44	39,728.18
Population Total	308,745,538	4,339,367
Population Density (people per square mile)	87.28	109.23
Population Percentage Change (April 1, 2000, to April 1, 2010)	9.7%	7.4%
White Persons (percent)	72.4%	87.8%
Black Persons (percent)	12.6%	7.8%
American Indian and Alaska Native Persons (percent)	0.9%	0.2%
Asian Persons (percent)	4.8%	1.1%
Native Hawaiian and Other Pacific Islander Persons (percent)	0.2%	0.1%
Some Other Race (percent)	6.2%	1.3%
Persons Reporting Two or More Races (percent)	2.9%	1.7%
Persons of Hispanic or Latino Origin (percent)	16.3%	3.1%
Not of Hispanic or Latino Origin (percent)	83.7%	96.9%
Median Household Income	$52,029	$41,489
Percentage of People Age 25 or Over Who Have Graduated from High School	80.4%	74.1%

*All figures are based on the 2010 United States Census, with the exception of the last two items.

How to Improve My Community

Strong communities make strong states. Think about what features are important in your community. What do you value? Education? Health? Forests? Safety? Beautiful spaces? Government works to help citizens create ideal living conditions that are fair to all by providing services in communities. Consider what changes you could make in your community. How would they improve your state as a whole? Using this concept web as a guide, write a report that outlines the features you think are most important in your community and what improvements could be made. A strong state needs strong communities.

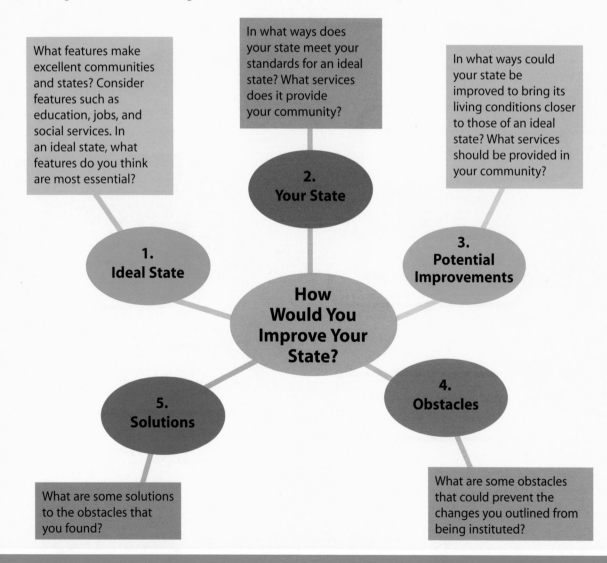

What features make excellent communities and states? Consider features such as education, jobs, and social services. In an ideal state, what features do you think are most essential?

In what ways does your state meet your standards for an ideal state? What services does it provide your community?

In what ways could your state be improved to bring its living conditions closer to those of an ideal state? What services should be provided in your community?

2.
Your State

1.
Ideal State

3.
Potential
Improvements

How
Would You
Improve Your
State?

5.
Solutions

4.
Obstacles

What are some solutions to the obstacles that you found?

What are some obstacles that could prevent the changes you outlined from being instituted?

Exercise Your Mind!

Think about these questions and then use your research skills to find the answers and learn more fascinating facts about Kentucky. A teacher, librarian, or parent may be able to help you locate the best sources to use in your research.

1 What is believed to have been the inspiration behind Kentucky's state song?

2 Which popular sandwich was first served in Louisville?

3 What was basketball coach Adolph Rupp's nickname?

4 What is the country's largest annual firework display?

5 What two families were involved in a famous Appalachian feud?

6 Which Kentucky city is built within a meteor crater?

7 When did the first Thoroughbred arrive in Kentucky?

8 Who was the state's first woman governor?

Words to Know

blaze: to make distinctive signs, such as chipping the bark on trees, to mark a trail route

bullion: bars of gold or silver

cavalry: troops mounted on horseback

commonwealth: a nation or state in which ultimate authority rests with the people

communal: relating to a community in which everything is shared

dressage: precise movements carried out by a horse in response to signals from its rider

equestrian: relating to horseback riding

floodplains: flat plains alongside a river or stream that flood frequently

hydroelectric: relating to the production of electricity by moving water

mandolin: a stringed musical instrument that has a pear-shaped wooden body and a fretted neck

migratory: characterized by traveling back and forth between locations depending on the season

rural: relating to the country

Thoroughbred: a breed of horse that originated in England and that is known for its racing ability

tributary: a stream or river that flows into a larger stream or river or into a lake

urban: relating to the city

vibraphone: a percussion instrument that looks like a xylophone

Index

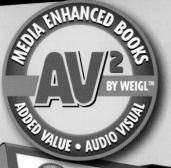

Log on to www.av2books.com

AV² by Weigl brings you media enhanced books that support active learning. Go to www.av2books.com, and enter the special code found on page 2 of this book. You will gain access to enriched and enhanced content that supplements and complements this book. Content includes video, audio, web links, quizzes, a slide show, and activities.

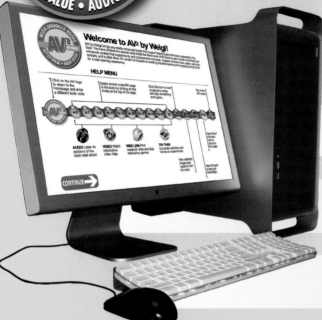

Audio
Listen to sections of the book read aloud.

Video
Watch informative video clips.

Embedded Weblinks
Gain additional information for research.

Try This!
Complete activities and hands-on experiments.

WHAT'S ONLINE?

Try This!	Embedded Weblinks	Video	EXTRA FEATURES
Test your knowledge of the state in a mapping activity.	Discover more attractions in Kentucky.	Watch a video introduction to Kentucky.	**Audio** Listen to sections of the book read aloud.
Find out more about precipitation in your city.	Learn more about the history of the state.	Watch a video about the features of the state.	
Plan what attractions you would like to visit in the state.	Learn the full lyrics of the state song.		**Key Words** Study vocabulary, and complete a matching word activity.
Learn more about the early natural resources of the state.			
Write a biography about a notable resident of Kentucky.			**Slide Show** View images and captions, and prepare a presentation.
Complete an educational census activity.			**Quizzes** Test your knowledge.

AV² was built to bridge the gap between print and digital. We encourage you to tell us what you like and what you want to see in the future.

Sign up to be an AV² Ambassador at www.av2books.com/ambassador.